A Guide for Using

Roll of Thunder, Hear My Cry

in the Classroom

Based on the book written by Mildred Taylor

*This guide written by **Michael H. Levin***
*Illustrated by **Sue Fu***

Teacher Created Resources, Inc.
6421 Industry Way
Westminster, CA 92683
www.teachercreated.com
©1994 Teacher Created Resources, Inc.
Reprinted, 2005
Made in U.S.A.
ISBN 1-55734-439-6

Table of Contents

Introduction 3

Sample Lesson Plan 4

Before the Book (Pre-reading Activities) 5

About the Author 6

Book Summary 7

Vocabulary Lists 8

Vocabulary Activity Ideas 9

Section 1 (Chapters 1 through 3) 10
    • Quiz—What Do You Know?
    • Hands-On Project—Montage
    • Cooperative Learning Activity—Racial Segregation
    • Curriculum Connections—Reading Response Journals
    • Into Your Life—Observation

Section 2 (Chapters 4 and 5) 15
    • Quiz—What Do You Know?
    • Hands-On Project—Storytelling
    • Cooperative Learning Activity—Seed Sprouting Race
    • Curriculum Connections—Social Studies: Mississippi Facts
    • Into Your Life—Understanding How Prejudice Works

Section 3 (Chapters 6 and 7) 20
    • Quiz—What Do You Know?
    • Hands-On Project—Southern Cooking
    • Cooperative Learning Activity—Dialect and Non-standard English
    • Curriculum Connections—History: The Civil Rights Movement
    • Into Your Life—Prices During the Great Depression

Section 4 (Chapters 8 and 9) . . . . · 26
    • Quiz—What Do You Know?
    • Hands-On Project—Create Curriculum
    • Cooperative Learning Activity—Dealing with Bullies
    • Curriculum Connections—Science: King Cotton
    • Into Your Life—Detecting Gender and Racial Bias

Section 5 (Chapters 10 through 12): 31
    • Quiz—What Do You Know?
    • Hands-On Project—Art: Family Coat of Arms
    • Cooperative Learning—Trial of T.J.
    • Curriculum Connections—Quotation Marks and Dialogue
    • Into Your Life—Resources
    After the Book (Post-reading Activities)

After the Book (Post-reading Activities): 36
    Book Report Ideas 37
    Research Activity 38

Culminating Activities 39

Unit Test Options 42

Bibliography of Related Reading 45

Answer Key 46

Introduction

A good book can touch our lives like a good friend. Within its pages are words and characters that can inspire us to achieve our highest ideals. We can turn to it for companionship, recreation, comfort, and guidance. It can also give us a cherished story to hold in our hearts forever.

In *Literature Units*, great care has been taken to select books that are sure to become good friends!

Teachers who use this unit will find the following features to supplement their own valuable ideas.

- Sample Lesson Plans

- Pre-reading Activities

- A Biographical Sketch and Picture of the Author

- A Book Summary

- Vocabulary Lists and Suggested Vocabulary Activities

- Chapters grouped for study with each section including:

    - quizzes

    - hands-on projects

    - cooperative learning activities

    - cross-curricular connections

    - extensions into the reader's own life

- Post-reading Activities

- Book Report Ideas

- Research Activity

- Culminating Activities

- Three Different Options for Unit Tests

- Bibliography

- Answer Key

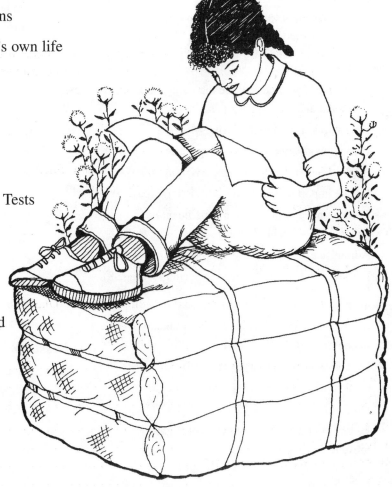

We are confident this unit will be a valuable addition to your planning, and we hope your students increase the circle of "friends" they have in books as you use our ideas!

Sample Lesson Plan

Each of the lessons suggested below can take from one to several days to complete.

Lesson 1

- Introduce and complete some or all of the pre-reading activities. (page 5)
- Read "About the Author" with your students. (page 6)
- Introduce the vocabulary list for Section 1. (page 8)

Lesson 2

- Read Chapters 1 through 3. As you read, place the vocabulary words in the context of the story and discuss their meanings.
- Do a vocabulary activity. (page 9)
- Make a montage. (page 11)
- Discuss racial segregation. (page 12)
- Begin "Reading Response Journals" (page 13)
- Discover something new as you walk to school. (page 14)
- Administer the Section 1 quiz. (page 10)
- Introduce the vocabulary list for Section 2. (page 8)

Lesson 3

- Read Chapters 4 and 5. Place the vocabulary words in context and discuss their meanings.
- Do a vocabulary activity. (page 9)
- Learn how to tell a good story. (page 16)
- Learn about and try growing seeds. (page 17)
- Locate important facts about Mississippi. (page 18)
- Conduct a week's classroom experiment on understanding prejudice. (page 19)
- Administer the Section 2 quiz. (page 15)
- Introduce the vocabulary list for Section 3. (page 8)

Lesson 4

- Read Chapters 6 and 7. Place the vocabulary words in context and discuss their meanings.
- Do a vocabulary activity. (page 9)
- Cook some regional dishes. (page 21)
- Discover dialect. (page 22)
- Learn about the history of the Civil Rights movement. (pages 23 and 24)

- Research the cost of food during the Great Depression. (page 25)
- Administer the Section 3 quiz. (page 20)
- Administer the vocabulary list for Section 4. (page 8)

Lesson 5

- Read Chapters 8 and 9. Place the vocabulary words in context and discuss their meanings.
- Do a vocabulary activity. (page 9)
- Create a curriculum. (page 27)
- Discuss how a bully can affect your life. (page 28)
- Find out about cotton. (page 29)
- Explore gender and racial bias. (page 30)
- Administer the Section 4 quiz. (page 26)
- Introduce the vocabulary list for Section 5. (page 8)

Lesson 6

- Read Chapters 10 through 13. Place the vocabulary words in context and discuss their meanings.
- Do a vocabulary activity. (page 9)
- Create a coat of arms. (page 32)
- Conduct a trial. (page 33)
- Practice punctuating dialogue. (page 34)
- Write for information about stopping various types of discrimination. (page 35)
- Administer the Section 5 quiz. (page 31)

Lesson 7

- Discuss any questions your students have about the story. (page 36)
- Assign book report and research activity. (pages 37 and 38)
- Begin work on one or more culminating activities. (pages 39-41)

Lesson 8

- Administer Unit Tests: 1, 2, and/or 3. (pages 42, 43, and 44)
- Discuss the test answers and possibilities.
- Discuss the students' enjoyment of the book.
- Provide a list of related reading for your students. (page 45)

Before the Book

Before you begin reading *Roll of Thunder, Hear My Cry* with your students, do some pre-reading activities to stimulate their interest and enhance their comprehension. Here are some activities that might work for your class.

1. Predict what the story might be about just by hearing the title.

2. Predict what the story might be about just by looking at the cover illustration.

3. Discuss other books by Mildred Taylor that students may have heard about or read.

4. Answer these questions:
   - Are you interested in:
     - stories about children and their brothers and sisters?
     - stories about the South?
     - stories with adventure and life-or-death struggles?
     - stories dealing with young people having experiences that make them become more mature?
     - stories that show a young person is capable of making important decisions and taking action?
     - stories that show that life continues even after tragic instances occur?
   - Why might a person think he/she has the right to kill someone?
   - How can racial prejudice affect a child's life?
   - How does a family remain strong when pressures are trying to tear it apart?
   - What is it like being the child of a teacher?
   - In a family with three boys and one girl, would the girl be treated differently?

5. Work in groups to create a factual and/ or fictional story about a family with three boys and one girl.

6. Write descriptions or brainstorm ideas about what makes a person strong or courageous in the face of tragedy. Determine what the source of such strength might be.

7. Use the picture on page 48 to introduce *Roll of Thunder, Hear My Cry* to your class. The picture can also be used as a journal cover for Reading Response Journals or as the centerpiece of a bulletin board display of student work.

About the Author

Mildred D. Taylor was born in Jackson, Mississippi, and educated in Toledo, Ohio. She went to the University of Toledo and received her Master's degree at the University of Colorado School of Journalism, in Boulder.

Ms. Taylor began her career with the Peace Corps, as an English and history teacher in Ethiopia for two years. She returned to the United States and was a Peace Corps recruiter. She then became a study skills co-ordinator for the University of Colorado Black Education Program.

Ms. Taylor published her first book, *Song of the Trees*, in 1975. Like *Roll of Thunder, Hear My Cry*, the book concerns the Logan family and—is told by Cassie, the first person narrator. *Roll of Thunder, Hear My Cry* was Ms. Taylor's second novel and it won the Newbery Medal in 1977. Her third book, *Let the Circle Be Unbroken*, published in 1982, continues the Logan story when Cassie is 11 and Stacey is 14. Two short novels, *Mississippi Bridge* (1987) and *The Friendship* (1990) are also about the Logans.

Ms. Taylor uses her early life as the inspiration for her stories. She credits her father for teaching her a truer history of the black people in the United States than she learned in school. Her family has a long history, stretching back into the days of slavery, in Mississippi, which is the setting of *Roll of Thunder, Hear My Cry*. In all of her books, Ms. Taylor draws her reader into the circle of an inspiring black family, full of strength and love. She shows us their traditions, heritage, and community.

When asked about her writing, Ms. Taylor replied,

> *"In* Roll of Thunder, Hear My Cry, *I included the teachings of my own childhood, the values and principles by which I and so many other black children were reared, for I wanted to show a different kind of black world from the one so often seen. I wanted to show a family united in love and self-respect; and parents, strong and sensitive, attempting to guide their children successfully, without harming their spirits, through the hazardous maze of living in a discriminatory society.... It is my hope that to the children who read my books, the Logans will provide those heroes missing from the schoolbooks of my childhood. Black men, women, and children of whom they can be proud. "*

(Quotations and information from *Something About the Author*, edited by Anne Commire, Gale Research, Detroit: 1971 and *Twentieth Century Children's Writers*, edited by D.L. Kirkpatrick, Saint Martin's Press, New York: 1983)

Roll of Thunder, Hear My Cry

by Mildred D. Taylor

(Penguin, 1976)

(Available in Canada, Penguin; UK and Australia: Penguin Ltd.)

Roll of Thunder, Hear My Cry is only one of Mildred Taylor's novels about the Logan family. All of these books about the Logans use the character of Cassie as the narrator. This novel takes place in western Mississippi, near Vicksburg, in 1933. It is basically a story of how Cassie learns about the inherent prejudice of whites against blacks in the South during the difficult times of the Depression.

Cassie Logan is a nine-year-old girl who lives with her mother, a seventh grade teacher, and her father, who must work on the railroad to supplement the family's farming income. Also in the house are Cassie's paternal grandmother, and three brothers—Stacey, 12, Christopher-John, 7, and Little Man, 6. The Logans own 400 acres, and are one of the few black landowning families in the community of sharecroppers. While Cassie is secure in the love of her close-knit family, she describes a year of perplexing and hurtful insults, some serious and some small.

Most serious is the rising tide of racial unrest brought on by the hard times of the Great Depression. "Night men" burn the men of the Berry family, killing one and badly disfiguring another. Papa returns with the gigantic, but kind and wise, Mr. Morrison to watch the family while he is away. The Wallaces, who are implicated in, but not prosecuted for the burnings, own a store where they encourage the black children to drink and gamble. With the help of Mr. Jamison, a white lawyer, Mama organizes a boycott of the Wallace's store. This costs Mama her teaching position.

"Night men" attack Papa while he, Stacey, and Mr. Morrison are returning from Vicksburg with supplies. Papa suffers a broken leg which keeps him from returning to the railroad. The situation becomes worse when Harlan Granger, a white plantation owner who wants the Logan land, persuades the bank to call in their mortgage. Uncle Hammer, who works in Chicago, must sell his silver Packard to pay off the debt. The novel ends with the near-lynching of T. J. Avery, a neighbor just a year older than Stacey, who is framed by some white youths. Papa sets fire to his field of cotton which adjoins the Granger plantation. This diverts the mob and the entire community works together to save the crops.

Cassie, a resourceful child, must deal with all the events and attempt to sort out her place in this world. The novel concludes with Cassie still searching, but with the help of her strong and caring family, it seems as though she will rise above the indignities of the segregated society.

Vocabulary

On this page are vocabulary lists which correspond to each sectional grouping of chapters. Vocabulary activity ideas can be found on page 9 of this book.

SECTION 1

Chapters 1-3

corduroy	meticulous(ly)
exasperation	concession
admonish(ed)	raucous
trudge(d)	pensive(ly)
ornate	outwit
dense	tormentor
loitering	knell
temerity	venison
tantrum	imperiously
resiliency	stealth(ily)
flirting	lynched

SECTION 2

Chapters 4 and 5

aloof	discourse
feign(ed)	engross(ed)
nauseous	vague(ly)
glint	subdue(d)
malevolent(ly)	dense(ly)
river(ed)	interject(ed)
falter(ed)	subtle
emphatic	proprietor(s)
envision(ed)	mercantile

SECTION 3

Chapters 6 and 7

audible	bridge (v.)
chignon	languid(ly)
apprehensive	goad(ed)
placid	boycott
condone(d)	sulk(ed)
obedience	frustration
inaudible	interminable

SECTION 4

Chapters 8 and 9

reassurance	irritably
saunter(ed)	generate(d)
seep	pneumonia
comprehend(ing)	scowl
indignant	suspiciousl(y)
feign(ed)	rile

SECTION 5

Chapters 10-12

despondent(ly)	reproach(fully)
scheme	desolate(ly)
interminable	acrid
urgency	persistent
humdrum	despicable
crescendo	flimsy

Vocabulary Activity Ideas

You can help your students learn and retain the vocabulary in *Roll of Thunder, Hear My Cry* by providing them with interesting vocabulary activities. Here are some ideas to try.

❑ People of all ages like to make and solve puzzles. Ask your students to make their own **Crossword Puzzles** or **Wordsearch Puzzles** using the vocabulary words from the story.

❑ Challenge your students to a **Vocabulary Bee**! This is similar to a spelling bee; but, in addition to spelling each word correctly, the game participants must correctly define the words as well.

❑ Play **Vocabulary Concentration**. The goal of this game is to match vocabulary words with their definitions. Divide the class into groups of 2-5 students. Have students make two sets of cards the same size and color. On one set have students write their vocabulary words. On the second set have them write the definitions. All cards are mixed together and placed face down on a table. A player picks two cards. If the pair matches the word with its definition, the player keeps the cards and takes another turn. If the cards don't match, they are returned to their places face down on the table, and another player takes a turn. Players must concentrate to remember the locations of the words and their definitions. The game continues until all matches have been made. This is an ideal activity for free exploration time.

❑ Have your students practice their writing skills by creating sentences and paragraphs in which multiple vocabulary words are used correctly. Ask them to share their **Compact Vocabulary** sentences and paragraphs with the class.

❑ Ask your students to create paragraphs which use the vocabulary words to present **History Lessons** that relate to the time period of the novel.

❑ Challenge your students to use a specific vocabulary word from the story at least **Ten Times in One Day**. They must keep a record of when, how, and why the word was used!

❑ As a group activity, have students work together to create an **Illustrated Dictionary** of the vocabulary words.

❑ Play **20 Clues** with the entire class. In this game, one student selects a vocabulary word and gives clues one by one about this word, until someone in the class can guess the word.

❑ Play **Vocabulary Charades**. In this game, vocabulary words are acted out.

You probably have many more ideas to add to this list. Try them! See students' vocabulary interest and retention increase.

What Do You Know?

Answer the following questions about Chapters 1, 2, and 3.

1. List the four Logan children and their ages.

_____

_____

2. The Logan land was once part of the Granger plantation. How did the Logan family get their land? What crop do they raise?

_____

3. In what state does the family live and in what year?

_____

4. Why must Papa work at another job? What is the work and where does he do it?

_____

_____

5. What does the driver of the school bus like to do to the black children who must walk to school?

_____

_____

6. Why does Little Man throw his school book onto the floor and stomp on it?

_____

_____

7. What does Mama do to the books for her seventh-grade class?

_____

_____

8. Describe Mr. Morrison. Why does Papa bring him to stay with the family?

_____

_____

9. What was the cause of John Henry Berry's death?

_____

10 What do Stacey, Cassie, and their brothers do in revenge for the continual school bus episodes?

_____

_____

Montage

As you read about Cassie's family you will probably make comparisons with your own family. Are you also the only girl in a family of boys? Maybe your family is the opposite, and you are the only boy in a family of girls. Or perhaps you are an only child. These differences in family structure play a part in making us who we are.

How about Cassie's "neighborhood"? Can you see any similarities between where she lives and where you live? Most of us live in cities. Cassie lives on a farm. Can you find anything similar about your trip to school and Cassie's description of hers?

Keeping Cassie's family and neighborhood in mind, make a montage of your family and community. A montage is a picture made up of many separate pictures. This montage should tell the viewer about your family and/or your community. In addition to pictures, you can also use drawings, maps, newspaper clippings, and other items.

Here are some other ideas for your montage:

- Look in the telephone book. Find out whether any people have the same last name as yours. Copy part of that page for your montage.

- Include a story of how your community got its name.

- Ask your family about some interesting incident that happened to them in the community or in the history of the family. Include a story about it.

- Take some pictures of people, places, and things in your neighborhood or community. Add them to your montage.

Visit one or more of the following places in your community. Get some information from someone who works there about what they do. Explain why the place is important to you and your family. Take pictures!

- town hall

- firehouse

- police station

- recycling center

- place of worship

- library

- hospital

- park or recreation center

- water department

- day-care center

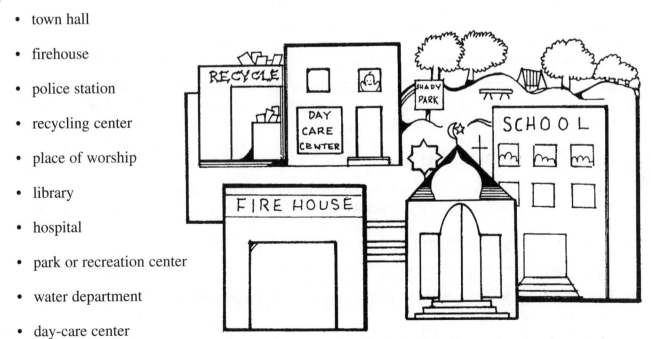

Racial Segregation

Cassie Logan went to a segregated school which means that children are separated from others on the basis of race. This is why the black children in the novel went to The Great Faith School. (Jefferson Davis was the President of the Confederate States when the southern part of the United States seceded from the rest of the country during the Civil War).

As late as 1954, when the Supreme Court voted to end segregation, 17 states and the District of Columbia still separated black and white students. This meant that 4 out of every 10 students in the United States went to segregated schools.

Divide your class into groups of four or five. Discuss the following in your group. Have one person record the answers for the group.

1. Imagine a time when black Americans and white Americans could not drink from the same drinking fountains. Or when they could not sit together in a restaurant or on a city bus. How do they think this made the black Americans feel?

   _____

   _____

2. The law of segregation said that it was permissible to separate children according to race as long as each received the same kind of education. What do you think this means?

   _____

   _____

3. In *Roll of Thunder, Hear My Cry* did the children of Great Faith Elementary receive an education equal to those at Jefferson Davis? Give examples to prove your point.

   _____

   _____

4. When the Supreme Court of the United States voted to end segregation, the justices said, "In these days it is doubtful that any child may reasonably be expected to succeed in life if he is denied the opportunity of an education ...To separate children from others of similar age and qualifications solely because of their race generates a feeling of inferiority as to their status in the community that may affect their hearts and minds in a way unlikely ever to be undone."

   Discuss what the justices of the Supreme Court meant when they decided to end segregation in schools. What does "affect their hearts and minds in a way unlikely ever to be undone" mean?

   _____

   _____

5. How do you think Cassie might be affected by going to a segregated school?

   _____

   _____

Reading Response Journals

One great way to ensure that the reading of *Roll of Thunder, Hear My Cry* becomes a personal experience for each student is to include the use of Reading Response Journals in your plans.

In these journals, students can be encouraged to respond to the story in a number of ways.

Here are a few ideas.

- Tell students that the purpose of the journal is to record their thoughts, ideas, observations, and questions as they read *Roll of Thunder, Hear My Cry*.

- Provide students with, or ask them to suggest, topics from the story that would stimulate writing. Here are a few examples from the chapters in Section 1:

  - Farm life in the Great Depression was different than living in today's world, whether one lives in the country or city. How is the Logan family's life different from ours?

  - The Logan family must live in fear because the white people in the community do not see black people as equal. Why do some people treat others with hate and distrust?

  - Stacey, Cassie, and their brothers purposely damage the school bus. They are furious because of all the times the driver embarrassed them. Were they justified? Is it ever justifiable to purposely ruin other people's property?

- After reading each chapter, students can write about one or more new things they learned in the chapter.

- Ask students to draw their responses to certain events or characters in the story, using blank pages in their journals.

- Tell students that they may use their journals to record "diary-type" responses that they may want to enter.

- Encourage students to bring their journal ideas to life. Ideas generated from their journal writing can be used to create plays, debates, stories, songs, poems, and art displays.

- Give students quotes from the novel and ask them to write their own responses. Make sure to do this before you go over the quotations in class. In groups they can list the different ways students can respond to the same quote.

Allow students time to write in their journals daily.

- Personal reflections will be read by the teacher, but no corrections or letter grades will be assigned. Credit is given for effort, and all students who sincerely try will be awarded credit. If a grade is desired for this type of entry, grade according to the number of journal entries completed. For example, if five journal assignments were given and the student conscientiously completes all five, then he or she receives an "A."

- Non-judgmental teacher notations should be made as you read journals to let the students know you are reading and enjoying their journals. Here are some types of responses that will please your journal writers and encourage them to write more.

  - "You have really found what's important in the story!"

  - "You write so clearly, I almost feel as if I am there."

  - "If you feel comfortable, I'd like you to share this with the class. I think they'll enjoy it as much as I have."

Observation

Cassie Logan and her brothers had an hour walk to school and back every day. On the way, Cassie observed many things: the cotton fields, pasture land, forest land, an ancient oak tree, and the reddish-brown earth. There were a few "man-made" objects too: the barbed-wire fence and the dreaded school bus.

Chances are, you don't have to walk so far to school. But whether you go on foot, by car, by bus, on a bike, or on a skateboard, there are many things for you to observe on your way.

Take five minutes and write all the things you can remember seeing on your way to school today.

_____

_____

_____

_____

_____

You probably think you've taken the trip to school so often that you couldn't possibly find anything new to see. Most of us don't really look with "new" eyes very often. We assume that everything stays pretty much the same. However, there are usually new things to see if we concentrate on finding them. Tomorrow on the way to school, spend time looking for something new. You can probably find at least five new things if you pay attention. Look at the tree you pass every day, but really don't see. What's special about it? How are the leaves shaped? Exactly what color is the bark? When you get to school, write down the new things you saw.

1. _____

2. _____

3. _____

4. _____

5. _____

You found more? Good for you. Write them down!

_____

_____

_____

_____

What Do You Know?

Answer the following questions about Chapters 4 and 5.

1. On the back of this paper, write a one paragraph summary of the major events that happened in these two chapters. Then complete the rest of the questions on this page.

2. After T.J. goes inside the Logan's house to get his cap, what do the children find him doing?

3. Why does Stacey feel some resentment toward Mr. Morrison, at first?

4. Why does Stacey go to the Wallace's store?

5. Mr. Morrison says he is not going to tell Stacey's mother about the children going to the Wallace's store. However, what does Mr. Morrison expect Stacey to do?

6. Why is Big Ma so proud of her late husband, Paul Edward?

7. Mama takes her children to see the Berrys. What point is she trying to make the children understand?

8. In what way does Mr. Wade Jamison, the lawyer, remind Cassie of her father?

9. Why does Cassie become so angry at Mr. Barnett?

10. Considering what has been happening between the races in their area, why does Big Ma make Cassie apologize to Lillian Jean Simms again?

Storytelling

In the introduction to *Roll of Thunder, Hear My Cry,* Mildred Taylor talks about her father as "a master storyteller." Several times during the novel, the author has characters describing their past to the Logan children. In Chapter 4, for example, Big Ma tells Cassie about how she and her husband bought the Logan property. She impresses upon Cassie why the land is so important to the family.

Everybody has a story to tell. It may be a story about family, special interests, or life in general. When you listen to someone talk about his or her life, you are participating in oral history. Usually this history is not written down, but is passed from one generation to another by storytelling. There are so many stories in a family that are just waiting to be discovered!

Listen to the stories of others. Ask older relatives or neighbors to tell you the stories of their lives. If you have a tape recorder, tape the stories. It is best to have a written set of questions to start the conversation or keep it going. Here are a few examples:

- Do you have a big family? How did you get along with your sisters and brothers?

- What kind of rules did you have around your house when you were young? Do you think they were good rules? What sort of things did your parents not allow you to do?

- Describe a meal and/or holiday when you were a child. Perhaps there is a special recipe or tradition you could share.

- What subjects did you study in school? What books do you remember reading?

- What games did you enjoy most when you were my age?

- Describe a special event that stands out in your mind.

Add any other questions you want to ask. Tell the class one of the interesting stories.

Humorous Stories

Ask several family members or neighbors, both young or old, to tell a funny story. Make a booklet where you write down the stories and illustrate them. Share your favorite story with the class.

Become a Storyteller

Pick two or three of your favorite stories and practice telling them without notes. Have a storytelling hour when you tell the stories to your class. If you act them out with some pantomime, they will be more interesting.

For the teacher: As you do these activities, your class will probably have questions about storytelling. Contact your local library and find out about inviting an amateur or professional storyteller to class. This will open up a special world of expression that has been all but lost in our modern world where we rarely get to listen to a good story told well.

Seed Sprouting Race

Cassie and Stacey go with Big Ma into the small town of Strawberry to sell milk and eggs. Living on a farm, the Logan family probably raised much of their own food. Although their main crop was cotton, they probably raised all of the vegetables they ate. During the Great Depression, many families in the cities, as well as in the country, had to raise their own vegetables because they could not afford to buy them in the stores.

In this cooperative activity you will learn which sort of plants grow most quickly. It will be an interesting experiment for your class, especially if each group uses different seeds.

Divide the class into groups of two, three, or four.

You'll need six kinds of seeds, one egg carton split in half, toothpicks, strips of paper, glue, potting soil, and water. Follow these directions:

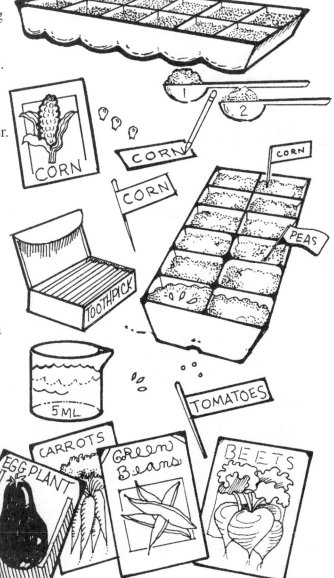

1. Put about two tablespoons (30 mL) of potting soil in each section of the egg carton.

2. Take one, two, or three seeds from a package. Put one kind of seed in each section. Cover the seeds with more soil, filling the section.

3. Write the name of the seed on a strip of paper. Glue the paper strip onto a toothpick. Stick toothpick in the soil.

4. Sprinkle section with water.

5. Repeat for the other five sections with different seeds in each section. Be very careful not to mix seeds.

6. Add a teaspoon (5 mL) of water everyday.

7. See which seeds sprout first. You can make a chart noting the different rates of growth.

8. Try planting your sprouting seeds outside.

Mississippi Facts

Directions: Use appropriate reference books to locate the following information about the state of Mississippi.

Population: _____ (ranks _____ in population)

Area: _____ square miles (ranks _____ in size)

Capital: _____

(How many people live in the capital city?_____)

State Nickname: _____

State Flower: _____

State Motto:_____

Highest Point in Mississippi: _____

Lowest Point in Mississippi:_____

Time Zone:_____

Three largest cities and their populations:

    1. _____

    2. _____

    3. _____

Vicksburg

Find the city of Vicksburg on a map of Mississippi. This small city is near the middle of Mississippi's western border. It is just west of the fictional Strawberry in the novel.

- Vicksburg is next to what river? _____

- What state is on the other side of the river? _____

- What state is about 60 miles (96.5 km) northeast of Vicksburg? _____

- What important city is 40 miles (64.3 km) east of Vicksburg?_____

- What city might our 42nd President be interested in visiting about 30 miles east of Vicksburg? _____

Understanding How Prejudice Works

While serious "hate" crimes are still committed today around the world, many children—in various locales—might not have any experience with, or understanding of, the intrinsic nature of prejudice and bias. The following exercise is designed to help all students "feel" the emotions which result from hate-motivated behavior. Plan for the exercise to take one school week. This will include: planning for; putting into action; discussing and doing follow-up. Adapt the activities to best suit your classroom situation.

Divide the class into half (or thirds). Each group is given a different-colored ribbon to wear for the duration of the exercise. For one entire day, students wearing one of the colors will be segregated, shunned, restricted in their activities, and discriminated against. The next day, a group wearing a different color ribbon will be targeted.

Each group makes up its own specific rules for discriminating against another group: the "others" must always go to the end of the line; can't sit in the shade at recess; can only drink from one certain water fountain, etc. The teacher might be amazed to observe how quickly the children can come up with their own ideas for unfair treatment of their fellow classmates.

During this week have children do the following activities:

1. Find articles in the newspaper and news magazines of racially motivated incidents presently taking place anywhere in the world.

   Discuss; put articles on a bulletin board where all can read them.

2. Encourage children to write daily in their journals about their feelings concerning the experiment.

3. Ask the class to discuss how "name-calling" makes the victim feel. Even if the victim knows the caller is ignorant, why does the name-calling make the victim angry and upset?

4. At the end of the week, have a class discussion about how the children felt when they were being discriminated against. Make a list of the "feelings" students describe. Discuss how having those feelings might influence someone's quality of life.

5. What can you do to help the races get along better?

What Do You Know?

Answer the following questions about Chapters 6 and 7.

1. On the back of this paper, write a one paragraph summary of the major events that happened in these two chapters. Then complete the rest of the questions on this page.

2. Whose car does Stacey and Cassie think is in their barn? Whose car is it?

   _____

3. Why does Mr. Morrison go after Uncle Hammer?

   _____

   _____

4. How does Mama explain Mr. Simm's behavior to Cassie?

   _____

   _____

5. How does T.J. trick Stacey into giving him the new coat?

   _____

   _____

6. What does the Logan family eat for their Christmas dinner?

   _____

   _____

7. Mr. Morrison tells the Logans about what happened to his family one Christmas when he was only six years old? Summarize what occurred.

   _____

   _____

8. Why do you think the Logan children were so excited about the books they received on Christmas?

   _____

   _____

9. Why does Jeremy bring over a present of nuts for the Logan family and a flute for Stacey?

   _____

   _____

10 Why does Mr. Jamison decide to help the black people buy their food and supplies in Vicksburg?

   _____

   _____

Southern Cooking

In Chapter 7, Cassie describes the food for the Logan family Christmas. "By the dawn, the house smelled of Sunday: chicken frying, bacon sizzling, and smoked sausages baking. By evening, it reeked of Christmas. In the kitchen sweet-potato pies, egg-custard pies, and rich butter pound cake cooled; a gigantic coon ...baked in a sea of onions, garlic, and fat orange-yellow yams; and a choice sugar-cured ham ...awaited its turn in the oven."

Southern cooking is one of the unique regional cuisines of the United States, yet it really is several cuisines. Southern can mean Creole, Cajun, Tex-Mex, soul food and barbecues.

Southern Ambrosia

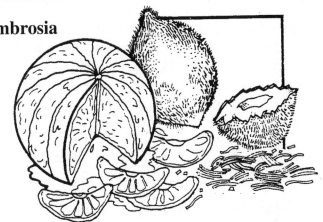

4 large sweet seedless oranges
1 cup (240 mL) shredded coconut
⅓ cup (80 mL) confectioner's sugar

Peel the oranges. Slice or section them with a knife. Put them in a bowl. Add the coconut and mix gently. Sprinkle with confectioner's sugar and chill until ready to eat.

Pecan Waffles

Use ready-made batter, or have the class make their own. Add ½ cup (120 mL) finely ground pecans for each 10 medium sized waffles. Pour mixture on surface of an electric waffle iron and cook according to manufacturer's instructions. (This will be a special treat for those who have never seen a waffle iron "in action.")

Homemade Peach Ice Cream

This will be an experience for many of the students who have never seen an ice cream freezer. Most of the freezers will be electric, but if you can get a hand-cranked type, the students will each feel they had a "hand" or "arm" in making the ice cream.

Follow the directions from the manufacturer. Any flavor will be enjoyed, but peach is especially delicious and "southern."

Sweet Potatoes

If you have access to an oven, bake some sweet potatoes and serve with a bit of butter. These are definitely southern and Cassie mentions eating them in the book. (NOTE: Sweet potatoes are native to the United States, but yams are not. Sometimes the dark-orange yam is called a "sweet potato." The true sweet potato is lighter in color.)

Dialect and Non-standard English

In Chapter 6, Cassie says, "Mama, he got something else he gotta do." Would you give this same information using the same words as Cassie? Maybe you would say, "Ma, there's sumpin' else he's got to do," or "Mother, he has to do something else." All of these sentences give the same information. However, the place where we were raised and the people we listened to as children give us our own special way of speaking.

Dialect is defined as a manner of speaking that is characteristic of a certain group or of the people of a certain geographical region. Dialects may differ from one another in the way vocabulary, pronunciation, and grammar is used. As in most countries, one dialect has become dominant. In America, this is called Standard English and can be heard from news broadcasters. Most people, however, speak a different dialect. Some writers, such as Mark Twain, Langston Hughes, and Mildred Taylor, use dialect in the dialogue of their writings in order to let the reader know how the character would actually sound.

In groups of two or three, read each of the expressions below and determine how it might be said in Standard English.

Example: "He was just a-settin' quiet-like" means "He was just sitting quietly."

(New England)	1. Didn't aim to tote it the whole way.
(New England)	2. Can't for the life of me understand.
(New York)	3. He was givin' me the one-two look with his eyes.
(New York)	4. He's the type person who lies.
(Southern)	5. He run off every which way.
(Southern)	6. If I had my druthers, I'd go.

Pick out five examples of dialect from *Roll of Thunder, Hear My Cry*. Write them down and have your group put them into Standard English.

_____

_____

_____

_____

_____

_____

The Civil Rights Movement

For black people, Mississippi in 1933 was a very difficult place to be. There were not equal rights for all people in law or in fact. It is often believed that black people were given equal rights after Abraham Lincoln signed the Emancipation Proclamation and the states re-united after the Civil War. This was not the case, however, especially in the South.

The following is a brief history of the Civil Rights Movement in the United States. It can be used to stimulate discussion or encourage students to do further research.

1863 (January 1)   Lincoln signed Emancipation Proclamation stating, "All people held as slaves" in the rebel states would be "thenceforward and forever, free."

1875   Congress passed a Civil Rights Act which stated that "citizens of every race and color" were entitled "to equal enjoyment of the accommodations of inns, public conveyances on land and water, theaters and other places of public amusement."

1867   Ku Klux Klan formed in Nashville, Tennessee, for "the maintenance of the supremacy of the white race." Within a year, this "invisible empire" had spread throughout the South.

1890   Laws passed in Southern states, requiring literacy tests or poll taxes, prevented blacks from voting. A white registrar could require a voter applicant to "explain" a section of the state constitution. This prevented most blacks from voting until 1965.

1896   The U.S. Supreme Court allowed states to segregate the races with the idea of "separate but equal" facilities. This allowed states to pass segregation laws which were called "Jim Crow" laws.

1901   Last black Congressman, George H. White of North Carolina, retired from the House of Representatives. Twenty-two black Southerners served in Congress in the years following the Civil War. Another black would not serve until 1920.

1910   W.E.B. DuBois and a committee of forty founded the NAACP (National Association for the Advancement of Colored People).

The Civil Rights Movement *(cont.)*

1900-1931   Almost 2,000 people were lynched in the United States. The vast majority occurred in the South and most of the victims were black. Much of these lynchings were the direct result of the rise of the Ku Klux Klan. By 1922, the NAACP began running advertisements that made the country aware of this outrage.

1939   Black performer Marian Anderson was not allowed to sing at Constitution Hall in Washington, D.C. Thousands, both black and white, came to hear her sing in front of the Lincoln Memorial in Washington, D.C.

1941-1945   Over one million black Americans fought in World War II. But the armed services were still "Jim Crow." Black groups worked to finally abolish this segregation in 1948.

1954   The Supreme Court declared that "separate but equal" in education is unlawful. It took more than ten years for desegregation to become a fact throughout the country.

1955   Bus boycotts in Montgomery, Alabama, signaled the end of the "Jim Crow" laws. Martin Luther King, Jr. assumed leadership of the Civil Rights Movements.

1963   One hundred years after Lincoln signed the Emancipation Proclamation, a quarter million Americans marched on Washington, D.C., to demand equal rights. King delivers his "I Have a Dream" speech.

1964-1966   Thousands of volunteers from all over the country travelled to the South to register blacks to vote.

1964   Civil Rights ensured restaurants, hotels, and other businesses would serve the general public without regard to race, color, religion, or national origin.

1965   Voting Rights Act outlawed voting literacy tests.

1966   Supreme Court prohibiteded poll taxes in state and local elections.

1968   Martin Luther King, Jr. was assassinated in Memphis, Tennessee.

1968   Civil Rights Act outlawed discrimination in rental of housing.

America's Great Economic Depression of the 1930s

The setting of *Roll of Thunder, Hear My Cry* is Mississippi in 1933. This was during the worst Depression of modern economic times. The Depression affected everyone in the United States, as well as most countries in the world. There were many people out of work and money was very scarce.

Below are some grocery items and prices from August 1933, (from an ad for the A & P grocery store in Bellevue, Ohio). On your next trip to the market, find out how much each of these items costs today and write the price on the blank lines.

		1933	Today
Soap	10 bars	27 cents	_____
Spaghetti	24 oz. (227 g)	17 cents	_____
Potatoes	10 lbs. (4.54 kg)	29 cents	_____
Oranges	2 dozen	35 cents	_____
Doughnuts	1 dozen	15 cents	_____
Coffee	1 lb. (454 g)	25 cents	_____
Ground beef	3 lbs. (1.36 kg)	20 cents	_____
Hot dogs	3 lbs. (1.36 kg)	25 cents	_____
Bacon	1 lb. (454 g)	11½ cents	_____
Pork roast	1 lb. (454 g)	5½ cents	_____
Bread	16 oz. (454 g) loaf	6 cents	_____
Sugar	10 lb. (4.54 kg)	51 cents	_____
Salad dressing	quart	25 cents	_____
Spinach	2 large cans	25 cents	_____
Margarine	3 lbs. (1.36 kg)	25 cents	_____

Add up what a person would pay for 10 or more grocery items in 1933. Then, using the information you gathered, add the amounts for the same items a person would spend today.

How much more does a trip to the market cost today? (Twice as much? Five Times? Ten Times?) Use your information to figure this out.

Why are the items so much more costly today? Discuss the reasons for inflation.

What Do You Know?

Answer the following questions about Chapters 8 and 9.

1. On the back of this paper, write a one paragraph summary of the major events that happened in these two chapters. Then complete the rest of the questions on this page.

2. Why is Lillian Jean surprised when Cassie asks if she can carry her books?

_____

_____

3. What is Cassie's real reason for acting like a servant for Lillian Jean?

_____

_____

4. Do you feel that Cassie's plan for revenge on Lillian Jean was a good one? Explain.

_____

_____

5. Why did T.J. want to get Mrs. Logan into trouble?

_____

_____

6. What do you think is the real reason Kaleb Wallace and Harlan Granger have Mrs. Logan fired?

_____

_____

7. How are R.W. and Melvin Simms treating T.J.? Why?

_____

_____

8. Why does Mr. Avery tell the Logans he can no longer shop in Vicksburg?

_____

_____

9. What happens to Papa on the way back from Vicksburg?

_____

_____

10. What are Christopher-John and Little Man most afraid of when Papa comes home from Vicksburg?

_____

_____

Creating a Curriculum

A curriculum is the course of study offered at a school. It is also an outline of what should be included in the different courses. The superintendent of Mama's school was unhappy because the history she was teaching was not part of the curriculum accepted by the School Board. Mama did not think that the true history of the United States was being taught, especially when it came to the history of the black people.

Your teacher follows the curriculum of your school district also. Each teacher can teach the subject in his or her own style, but is required to follow guidelines. In some subjects the outline is very detailed; for others it is sketchy. Ask your teacher about the curriculum for your grade.

If you could plan the curriculum for your class, what subjects would you choose? How would you explain the importance of these classes? Fill in the page and construct your own curriculum.

1. What subjects your class studies are the most important to you? Explain why each is important.

   _____

   _____

   _____

2. Which subjects should be eliminated from your class this year? Explain why.

   _____

   _____

   _____

3. What subjects that are not taught should be added? Add these to your curriculum and explain the reason they should be part of your course of study.

   _____

   _____

   _____

4. Now that you have your curriculum, put subjects in the order they should be taught during the day. Also put down how many minutes should be scheduled each day for each subject. (If any of your students should be taught only one, two, or three days a week, list that information.)

   _____

   _____

   _____

   _____

Dealing With People Who Want To Do You Harm

In Chapter 8, Cassie begins a plan to pay Lillian Jean Simms back for humiliating her in Strawberry. Lillian Jean took advantage of her position in the "Jim Crow South" to make Cassie feel inferior. However, after the initial anger wore off, Cassie figures a way to get even.

Divide into groups of three or four. Choose one person to write down the thoughts your group discusses about the following topics. Use the back of this page, if necessary.

1. Discuss how and why Lillian Jean humiliates Cassie in Chapter 5.

   _____

2. In your group, discuss what you think of the way Cassie gets even.

   _____

3. Discuss how Cassie is wise enough to understand her "opponent" so well that she knows Lillian Jean will not tell anybody about what Cassie did.

   _____

4. Is Cassie's plan of retaliation successful? (Here you must discuss the way Lillian Jean reacts when the "game" is over.)

   _____

   _____

5. Although Cassie is stronger than Lillian Jean, the white girl acts like a bully in Strawberry because she knows the black girl probably will not hurt her. Discuss different ways a bully will "pick" on someone "weaker."

   _____

   _____

6. Many psychologists say that a bully acts the way he does because he feels bad about himself. A bully picks on others when there is something going on in his own life that he dislikes but cannot do anything about. Does your group think this is true about bullies? Discuss.

   _____

   _____

7. It doesn't matter why bullies act the way they do when it is you they are picking on. A bully can make a person's life miserable, especially when the victim cannot think of how to make the situation better. Discuss in your group what can be done to make a bully stop pestering a person.

   _____

   _____

King Cotton

When Mama loses her job, the Logans plant more cotton to partly make up for the loss of income. Cotton was the most important crop of the southern United States at the time the novel takes place. Find out about cotton by researching the following:

1. How does cotton grow? What does the plant look like?

2. The invention of the cotton gin made the planting of cotton profitable. What does the cotton gin do?

3. Cotton is frequently used as a material in clothing. What is special about cotton that makes it so comfortable to wear?

4. What is the boll weevil? What does it look like? Find a picture to share with the class.

5. How does the boll weevil destroy the cotton plant?

6. How is the boll weevil controlled?

7. What other pests are harmful to the cotton plant?

8. How is cotton farming harmful to the soil? What was done to keep the earth usable?

9. What is crop rotation? How was it important to the cotton farmers?

10 What are the synthetic fibers often used in place of cotton? How are they different from cotton? How does the manufacturing of synthetic fiber affect the cotton farmers?

11 How was the invention of the mechanical cotton picker helpful in saving cotton as an important U.S. crop?

12 One of the most important by-products of cotton is cottonseed oil. What is cottonseed oil used for?

13 On the back of this page, draw a picture of the cotton plant.

Detecting Gender And Racial Bias

Cassie Logan had to deal with racial bias from the Simms. The Logans also felt discrimination from Harlan Granger and others. Many people experience discrimination in their daily lives. Some of the discrimination is similar to what Cassie experienced— based on racial prejudice. Other discrimination is directed toward a person's gender. Read the following statements. Decide whether there is a bias or prejudice. Check the appropriate column.

	Gender Bias	Racial Bias	No Bias
1. Mr. Jones asked the strong boys to carry the dictionaries to the book room.			
2. The musicians practiced for the concert.			
3. Firemen must always be ready to react to the alarm.			
4. Hispanic children are naturally kind.			
5. Dr. Jones is a famous woman doctor.			
6. Boys are better in math than girls.			
7. Tall people have a better view of parades.			
8. Black people have more rhythm than white people.			
9. Women had to wait until 1920 to get the right to vote.			
10. Our forceful president has an attractive wife.			
11. More women than men watch soap operas.			
12. My dad has an important job, but my mom only stays home.			
13. Moms cook better than dads.			
14. My younger sister reads better than I do.			
15. Asian children are excellent students.			

Have a class discussion. Did everyone have the same answers? Write your own definitions of bias.

What Do You Know?

Answer the following questions about Chapters 10, 11, and 12.

1. On the back of this paper, write a two paragraph summary of the major events that happened in these three chapters. Then complete the rest of the questions on this page.

2. When Kaleb Wallace will not move his truck and let Mr. Morrison by with the wagon, what does Mr. Morrison do?

_____

3. Why do you think Jeremy spends so much time in his tree house?

_____

_____

4. What are some reasons Cassie likes the annual revival meeting?

_____

_____

5. How does Uncle Hammer raise the money to pay the mortgage?

_____

_____

6. Why does Cassie feel sorry for T.J. when he comes to the revival meeting?

_____

_____

7. Briefly describe what happened when T.J. and the Simmses go to the Barnett's store to get the pearl-handled pistol.

_____

_____

8. Who is able to stop the Wallaces from immediately killing T.J.?

_____

_____

9. Why do you think Papa starts the fire in his own cotton field?

_____

_____

10. At the end of the last chapter, why do you think Cassie cries for T.J., even though she never liked him?

_____

_____

Family Coat of Arms

Although Cassie has a difficult life in the racially divided Mississippi of 1933, she has the strong support of her family. There are many values that the Logan family share. Some are:

education	*caring*	*honesty*
love	*sense of history*	*completion of tasks*
importance of traditions	*self-respect*	*strength of beliefs*

Decide which of these are most important for a supportive family to share with each other. Perhaps you can think of others.

Design a coat of arms for the Logan family, using a visual interpretation of the different values. You could represent education by using a diploma or a book. Caring could be represented by a mother standing at the bedside of a sick child or a parent and child playing ball together. Fill in the form below with at least four different pictures.

Extension: Create a coat of arms for your family using at least four different pictures.

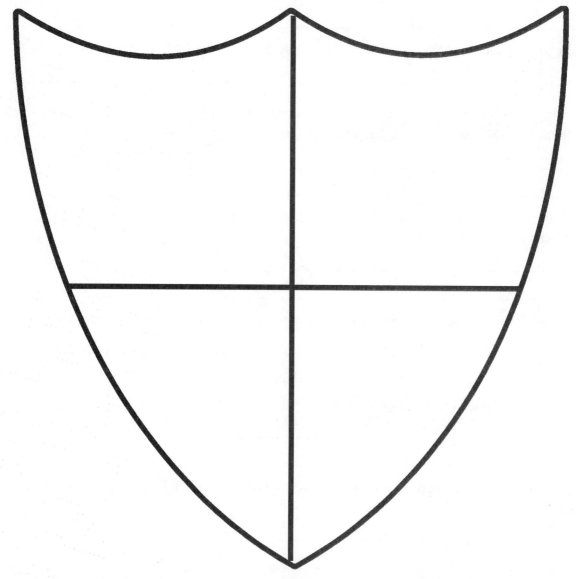

Trial of T.J.

At the end of *Roll of Thunder, Hear My Cry,* T.J. Avery is almost lynched for the murder of Mr. Barnett. He is saved by Mr. Jamison, the lawyer, but will still be tried for the crime. T.J. told Stacey and Cassie his version of what happened at the Barnett store.

Have a trial in your classroom and let a jury decide who is guilty and should go to jail for Mr. Barnett's murder. You will need the following characters.

People involved in the murder

- T.J. Avery

- R.W. Simms

- Melvin Simms

- Mrs. Barnett

Witnesses who can relate what they heard and saw

- Cassie

- Stacey

- Christopher-John

- Little Man

Involved after the murder

(can be called as witnesses, if needed)

- Kaleb Wallace

- Thurston Wallace

- Mr. Avery

- Mrs. Avery

- Claude Avery

Lawyers—need to work with the clients and call witnesses to prove their case.

- Defense lawyer—for T.J. (Mr. Jamison could be T.J.'s lawyer or be called for a witness to the beating of the Averys, although he arrived immediately after it was over). This lawyer must try and prove T.J. innocent of Mr. Barnett's murder. He or she needs to call witnesses who will help prove this. This person needs to completely understand what occurred in the novel.

- Prosecution lawyer—this lawyer tries to prove that T.J. was guilty of Mr. Barnett's murder. He or she needs to call witnesses who will help prove that T.J. is guilty. This person must carefully understand what occurred in the novel.

- Judge—must keep the trial moving and stop lawyers from saying anything unfair or from trying to get witnesses to say anything that cannot be proved. This person must understand the novel extremely well and must not be afraid to tell the lawyers how to conduct themselves.

- Jury—any student without a part will sit on the jury. The jury should pick a leader. After the jury hears all of the testimony, they must vote and decide whether T.J. is guilty. Their decision should be based on what occurs during the trial, not what happened in the novel.

Quotation Marks and Dialogue

Look at this excerpt from Chapter 10.

> *As we neared the church, Papa met us and embraced Uncle Hammer. I wasn't expecting you to come all the way down here. You expecting me to send that much money by mail? Could've wired it. Don't trust that either. How'd you get it? Borrowed some of it, sold a few things, he said with a shrug. Then he nodded at Papa's leg. How'd you do that? Papa's eyes met Uncle Hammer's and he smiled faintly. I was sort of hoping you wouldn't ask that. Uh-huh. Papa, I said, Uncle Hammer sold the Packard. Papa's smile faded. I didn't mean for that to happen, Hammer.*

This dialogue is not impossible to figure out, but imagine having to do it every time there was dialogue in a story. Most of us would give up before very long. The reason for quotation marks and dialogue punctuation is to make reading easier for the reader.

There are really very few rules to remember when using dialogue.

1. Skip a line and indent every time one person stops speaking and another one begins.

2. All words spoken out loud have quotation marks around them—even if only one word is spoken.

3. Words that help a reader to understand, such as *said Cassie* do not have quotation marks.

4. Punctuation marks at the end of a spoken sentence go inside the quotation marks.

Using those rules, see how much they help by taking another look at the speeches that began the page.

> *As we neared the church, Papa met us and embraced Uncle Hammer. "I wasn't expecting you to come all the way down here."*
>
> *"You expecting me to send that much money by mail?"*
>
> *"Could've wired it."*
>
> *"Don't trust that either. "*
>
> *"How'd you get it?"*
>
> *"Borrowed some of it, sold a few things," he said with a shrug. Then he nodded toward Papa's leg, "How'd you do that?"*
>
> *Papa's eyes met Uncle Hammer's and he smiled faintly, "I was sort of hoping you wouldn't ask that." "Uh-huh."*
>
> *"Papa," I said, "Uncle Hammer sold the Packard."*
>
> *Papa's smile faded. "I didn't mean for that to happen, Hammer."*

Read the following excerpt from Chapter 12 and use the dialogue rules to make it easy for the reader to understand.

Stacey, you all right? I cried. What about T.J.? And C-Claude? stammered Christopher-John. And Little Man asked, Papa and Mr. Morrison, ain't they coming? Mama held up her hand wearily. Babies! Babies! Then she put her arm around Christopher-John. Claude's fine, honey, And, she said, looking down at Little Man, Papa and Mr. Morrison, they'll be coming soon. But T.J., Mama, I persisted. What about T.J.?

Resources

The Logan family, in 1933, had no place to turn to for help with the sort of discrimination they had to deal with. But today there are organizations that help people with all kinds of discrimination. Below are addresses you can write to for information on combatting prejudice and discrimination.

Age Discrimination

Center for the Study of Aging
706 Madison Avenue
Albany, NY 12208

The Gray Panthers
15 West 65th
Street New York, NY 10023

Civil Liberties and Human Rights

Children's Legal Rights Information and Training Program
2008 Hillyer Place
Washington, DC 20009

International League for Human Rights
432 Park Avenue South
New York, NY 10016

Office of Civil Rights, Department of Education
400 Maryland Avenue SW
Washington, DC 20202

The Handicapped/Physically Challenged

Canadian Council of the Blind
220 Dundas Street (Suite 610)
London, Ontario N6A 1H3

National Association for the Visually Handicapped
22 West 21st Street
New York, NY 10011

National Information Center for Handicapped Children and Youth with Disabilities
P.O. Box 1492
Washington, DC 20013

The Homeless/The Poor

National Coalition for the Homeless
105 East 22nd Street
New York, NY 10010

Office for Civil Rights, Department of Health and Human Services
330 Independence Ave. SW
Washington, DC 20231

Physical and Sexual Abuse

American Humane Association
9725 East Hampden
Denver, CO 80231

Childhelp/International
6463 Independence Avenue
Woodland Hills, CA 91370

Society for the Prevention of Cruelty to Children
161 William Street
New York, NY 10003

Race, Religion, National Origin

American Jewish Congress
15 East 84th Street
New York, NY 10028

Anti-Defamation League of B'nai Brith
823 U.N. Plaza
New York, NY 10017

Association of American Indian Affairs
95 Madison Avenue
New York, NY 10016

Congress of Racial Equality (CORE)
236 West 116th Street
New York, NY 10037

National Association for the Advancement of Colored People (NAACP)
144 West 125th Street
New York, NY 10027

National Conference of Christians and Jews
71 Fifth Avenue (Suite 1100)
New York, NY 10003

National Congress of American Indians
804 D Street NE
Washington, DC 20002

National Urban League
500 East 62nd Street
New York, NY 10021

Contact the government offices in your city, county and/or state.

Any Questions?

When you finished reading *Roll of Thunder, Hear My Cry*, did you have some questions that were left unanswered? Write them here.

_____

_____

_____

Now work in groups or by yourself to prepare possible answers for the questions you asked above or those printed below. When you finish, share your ideas with the class.

- Did Mama ever get her teaching job back?

- What happens to T.J.?

- Are R.W. and Melvin Simms ever charged with the murder of Mr. Barnett?

- Does Papa go back to work on the railroad?

- Does Mr. Morrison stay with the family?

- Are the Logans able to keep their land? If so, how?

- Is Jeremy ever accepted as a friend by the Logan family?

- Does the family ever discuss how the fire began?

- Is the Logan family able to send Cassie away to high school or college?

- What is Uncle Hammer's occupation?

- Is there ever peace between the whites and blacks so the Logan family does not have to live in fear?

- Do the black children and white children ever go to the same school?

- Will Cassie ever be able to control her temper?

- Do Lillian Jean and Cassie ever speak again?

- Does Mr. Jamison remain friends with the Logans?

- After Mama is fired, who takes her place? Describe Stacey's new teacher.

Book Report Ideas

There are numerous ways to report on a book once you have read it. After you have finished reading *Roll of Thunder, Hear My Cry*, choose one method of reporting on the book that interests you. It may be a way your teacher suggests, an idea of your own, or one of the ways mentioned below.

- **See What I Read?**

  This report is a visual one. A model of a scene from the story can be created, or a likeness of one or more of the characters from the story can be drawn or sculpted.

- **Time Capsule**

  This report should provide those people who will live at a future time with the reasons *Roll of Thunder, Hear My Cry* is such an outstanding book, and give those "future" people reasons why it should be read. Make a time capsule-type of design, and neatly print or write your reasons inside the capsule. You may wish to "bury" your capsule after you have shared it with your classmates. Perhaps someone will find it and read *Roll of Thunder, Hear My Cry* because of what you wrote!

- **Come to Life!**

  This report is one that lends itself to a group project. A size-appropriate group prepares a scene from the story for dramatization, acts it out, and relates the significance of the scene to the entire book. Costumes and props will add to the dramatization!

- **Into the Future**

  This report predicts what might happen if *Roll of Thunder, Hear My Cry* were to continue. It may take the form of a story in narrative or dramatic form, or a visual display.

- **Who or What?**

  This report is similar to "Twenty Questions." The reporter gives a series of clues about a character from the story in vague-to-precise, general-to-specific order. After all clues have been given, the identity of the mystery character must be deduced. After the character has been guessed, the same reporter presents another "Twenty Clues" about an event in the story.

- **A Character Comes To Life!**

  Suppose one of the characters in *Roll of Thunder, Hear My Cry* came to life and walked into your home or classroom. This report gives a view of what this character sees, hears, and feels as he or she experiences the world in which you live.

- **Sales Talk**

  This report serves as an advertisement to "sell" *Roll of Thunder, Hear My Cry* to one or more specific groups. You decide on the group to target and the sales pitch you will use. Include some kind of graphic in your presentation.

- **Literary Interview**

  This report is done in pairs. One student will pretend to be a character in the story, steeped completely in the personality of his or her character. The other student will play the role of a television or radio interviewer, trying to provide the audience with insights into the character's personality and life. It is the responsibility of the partners to create meaningful questions and appropriate responses.

Famous Mississippians

Besides Mildred Taylor, the author of *Roll of Thunder, Hear My Cry,* there are many other famous people born in the state of Mississippi.

Choose one person from the list below and present an oral report to the class.

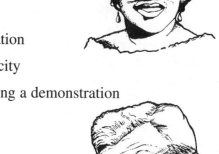

Leontyne Price

- Ralph Boston, track-and-field star
- Will Clark, professional baseball player
- Mart Crowley, playwright
- Bo Diddley, singer and guitar player
- Mike Espy, Secretary of Agriculture in the Clinton Administration
- Charles Evers, first black mayor of a racially-mixed southern city
- Medgar Evers, civil rights leader murdered in Mississippi during a demonstration
- William Faulkner, Nobel and Pulitzer Prize-winning author
- Ruth Ford, actress
- Fannie Lou Hamer, civil rights leader
- Jim Henson, puppeteer, creator of the Muppets
- James Earl Jones, Tony Award-winning actor
- B.B. King, blues musician
- James Meredith, first black student to attend University of Mississippi
- Archie Moore, world light-heavyweight champion
- Walter Payton, professional football player
- Leontyne Price, opera singer
- Charlie Pride, country-and-western singer
- Elvis Presley, rock-and-roll singer
- Pushmataha, Choctaw chief
- Jerry Rice, professional football player
- Richard Wright, author who wrote of racial prejudice he experienced
- Conway Twitty, country singer
- Muddy Waters, blues musician
- Ida B. Wells, civil rights leader who was born a slave
- Eudora Welty, Pulitzer Prize-winning author
- Tennessee Williams, Pulitzer Prize-winning playwright
- Oprah Winfrey, television personality and actress
- Tammy Wynette, country singer

William Faulkner

James Meredith

Elvis Presley

More by Mildred Taylor

There are two short novels—*The Friendship* and *Mississippi Bridge*—written by Mildred Taylor that are about the same characters found in *Roll of Thunder, Hear My Cry*. Either or both of the novels would make an excellent listening assignment for the class. Each novel is short and exciting with a strong and tragic climax. Use the summaries and questions below.

Before reading the book(s), ask students what they think this novel will be about. What can they surmise from the cover illustrations? While reading (stop where you wish), ask what thoughts they are having as you read. What do they predict will happen?

The Friendship

Cassie relates a trip to the Wallace's store, the place where her parents have forbidden them to go. There they meet their neighbor, Mr. Tom Bee, an old black man, calling the white store owner by his first name. Cassie understands that this kind of familiarity is not allowed. Mr. Bee tells the four Logan family members that he had once saved Mr. Wallace's life and had given him a home for some time. Wallace then told Mr. Bee that he could always call him by his first name. However, now Wallace feels Bee should not do this in front of others. Bee remembers the promise and continues to act "too familiar" with Wallace. Wallace ultimately shoots Bee in the leg to show his white customers that he is in control of the situation. Although on the ground and in pain, Bee continues to yell out Wallace's first name.

1. Why do the Logan children go to the Wallace's store?
2. Why does John Wallace believe he no longer owes Mr. Bee respect?
3. How did Mr. Bee save John Wallace's life?
4. Why does John Wallace shoot Tom Bee?
5. Why does Tom Bee keep shouting "John" at the end of the story?

Mississippi Bridge

This novel is narrated by Jeremy Simms, the ten-year-old white neighbor of the Logan children. Jeremy, sitting on the porch of the Wallace's store, watches as people board the weekly bus. He is joined by the Logan children as they watch their grandmother get on the bus. One person, Josias Williams, is also getting on the bus to travel to a promised job. A few minutes before, he had been verbally attacked by the white customers of the store because they felt it was "wrong" for a black man to have a job when white people were unemployed. When the bus is almost fully loaded, Jeremy hears the bus driver order the black passengers to get off because there were white people who wanted their seats. All the black passengers get off except for Josias. He is physically thrown from the bus. On the way home Jeremy and Josias witness the bus going off the bridge into a roaring river. Josias tries to save the passengers, but all do not survive. Jeremy attempts to understand the day's events.

1. What happens in the store concerning the wide-brim hat?
2. Why are the men in the store so cruel to Josias Williams?
3. Why are the black passengers forced off the bus?
4. What happens to the bus after it leaves the store?
5. Why does Josias try to help save the drowning passengers?

Sympathy

Listen as your teacher reads the following poem to the class.

Sympathy
by Paul Laurence Dunbar

I know what the caged bird feels, alas!
When the sun is bright on the upland slopes;
When the wind stirs soft through the springing grass,
And the river flows like a stream of glass;
When the first bird sings and the first bud opes,
And the faint perfume from its chalice steals—
I know what the caged bird feels!

I know why the caged bird beats his wing
Till its blood is red on the cruel bars;
For he must fly back to his perch; and cling
When he fain would be on the bough a-swing
And a pain still throbs in the old, old scars
And they pulse again with a keener sting—
I know why he beats his wing!

I know why the caged bird sings, ah me,
When his wing is bruised and his bosom sore,—
When he beats his bars and he would be free;
It is not a carol of joy or glee,
But a prayer that he sends from his heart's deep core,
But a plea, that upward to Heaven he flings—
I know why the caged bird sings!

— (Written in 1896. Dodd-Mead to Putnam to Breslow & Walker. All rights returned to the author.)

Part 1

Carefully read the poem again silently and then complete the following activities by yourself. Ideas are more important than writing.

1. What is your first response to the poem? Write down any thoughts, questions, or opinions you have.

2. On the left side of your paper, copy two lines from the poem that seem interesting. Opposite each line, make appropriate comments, such as what it means, what it reminds you of, what you don't understand, or how you feel about it.

3. Draw a representation of an open mind in which you insert symbols, images, words, or phrases of your own that express what the speaker of the poem is feeling. Make the open mind about as big as your hand.

4. Explain the meaning of the symbols, images, words, and phrases that you included in your open mind. Explain why you chose them.

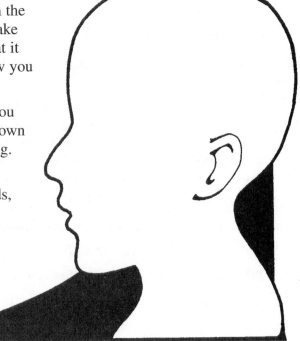

Sympathy *(cont.)*

Part 1 *(cont.)*

5. There are several important images in this poem. Select the image you feel is most important and explain why you feel this way.

6. Here is your chance to write anything you understand about the poem—what it means to you, what it makes you think about in your own life, or anything that relates to your reading of it.

When you finish, review your work in Part 1 and wait for directions to begin Part 2.

Part 2

Divide into groups of three or four. Discuss the poem. It is important that everyone in the group has a chance to participate. One person should volunteer to act as the leader. The leader should keep the discussion focused on the topic and see that everyone has an opportunity to speak. Each member should share in the discussion and take notes or write responses when the directions call for it. Please number your responses.

1. What was most memorable about the poem? Quickly jot down your ideas.

2. Now share these ideas orally with your group and record some new ideas presented by other people.

3. Share the symbols, images, words, and phrases that you drew in your open mind. Record some new ideas that other people presented. (Do not add to your open mind.)

4. The leader will read the last stanza of the poem aloud to the group. Think about the carol (song) that the bird sings. Write down your thoughts about why the song is more like a prayer. What is the bird praying for? Discuss your writing with the group.

5. Dunbar is really talking about a person who is not allowed to reach his or her full potential in life. Write how a person might behave who is kept from trying to do what he or she is capable of achieving.

When your group finishes, review your work in Part 2. Wait for directions to continue.

Part 3

Do this alone. Both ideas and writing are important.

Writing Situation: *In Roll of Thunder, Hear My Cry,* Cassie is often kept from achieving all that she can because of racial prejudice. This both hurts and confuses her.

Directions for Writing: Compare what happens in the poem to what occurs to Cassie in the novel. Think and write about the incidents where Cassie is a victim of prejudice and compare it to the way the bird feels in the poem.

Unit Test

Matching: Match the quote with the person who said it.

Cassie	Papa	Mama	T.J.
Jeremy	Little Man	Stacey	Mr. Jamison

1. _____ "Y'all go ahead and get dirty if y'all wanna...Me, I'm gonna stay clean."

2. _____ "See, if you was smart like me, Stacey, you'd use the old brain to get the questions on that big test comin' up. Just think, they probably just sittin' right here in this very room watin' to be discovered."

3. _____ "He'll be thirteen next month, honey, and he needs to be with me more. I can't take him with me on the railroad, but I can take him with me where I go around here. And I want him to know business...how to take care of it, how to take care of things when I ain't around."

4. _____ "Built it myself and I sleeps up there. Come these hot nights, I just climbs in my tree and it's like going into another world...Sometimes I think I can even see all the way over to y'all's place."

5. _____ "It will be easy enough for anyone to see whose responsibility it is, Daisy, by opening any seventh-grade book. Because tomorrow I'm going to'mess them up' too."

6. _____ "Jim Lee Barnett and his wife are still alive. Y'all let the sheriff and me take the boy. Let the law decide whether or not he's guilty."

7. _____ "Then Jack reared up, scared by the shot, and I—I couldn't hold him... and... and the wagon rolled over Papa's leg...It's m-my fault his leg's busted!"

8. _____ "Uh…excuse me, Mr. Barnett. I think you forgot but you was waiting on us, before you was waiting on this girl here, and we been waiting a good while now for you to get back."

True or False: Write true or false next to each statement below.

1. _____ Mama knows the real reason she was fired is because she was teaching history that wasn't in the textbook.

2. _____ Melvin and R.W. Simms are true friends to T.J.

3. _____ Uncle Hammer's car is almost exactly like the one Harlan Granger drives.

4. _____ Lillian Jean does not understand the point of Cassie pretending to be nice to her.

5. _____ Papa brings Mr. Morrison to live with the family to protect them from possible trouble from the white community.

Sequence: Put these events in order by number 1 to 5 on the lines.

_____ T.J. almost gets lynched

_____ Boycott of the Wallace's store

_____ Mama loses her teaching job

_____ Robbery of the Barnett's store

_____ Berry family is burned

Paragraphs: Answer the following in paragraph form on the back of this sheet.

1. Discuss some of the times when Cassie has trouble understanding the way she is treated by people outside of her family.

2. Discuss why Cassie knows never to talk about the circumstances of the fire in the cotton field.

Response

Explain the meaning of each of these excerpts from *Roll of Thunder, Hear My Cry.*

Chapter 1: *"You ain't never had to live on nobody's place but your own and long as I live and the family survives, you'll never have to. That's important. You may not understand that now, but one day you will. Then you'll see."*

Chapter 1: *"Mama laughed. 'If that's the case, Daisy, I don't think I need that little bit of food.'*

Chapter 2: *"The rest of us agreed; Papa always meant what he said—and he swung a mean switch."*

Chapter 3: *"We consequently found ourselves comical objects to cruel eyes that gave no thought to our misery."*

Chapter 4: *"Everyone knows they did it, and the Wallaces laugh about it, but nothing was ever done."*

Chapter 5: *"I whipped my hand from his. 'What's the matter with you? You know we was wrong!' Stacey swallowed to flush his anger, then said gruffly, 'I know it and you know it, but he don't know it, and that's where the trouble is."*

Chapter 6: *(Mama) "Baby, you had to grow up a little today. I wish...well, no matter what I wish. It happened and you have to accept the fact that in the world outside this house, things are not always as we would have them to be. "*

Chapter 7: *(Papa) "Now you could be right about Jeremy making a much finer friend than T.J. ever will be. The trouble is, down here in Mississippi, it costs too much to find out...So I think you'd better not try."*

Chapter 8: *"Then I turned and left the forest, not wanting to believe that Lillian Jean didn't even realize it had all been just a game."*

Chapter 9: *(Papa) "But that fig tree's got roots that run deep, and it belongs in that yard as much as that oak and walnut. It keeps on blooming, bearing good fruit year after year, knowing all the time it'll never get as big as them other trees.*

Chapter 10: *"Big Ma said to Mama, 'I sure wish Hammer could've stayed longer.' 'It's better he went, said Mama."*

Chapter 11: *(T.J.) "You my only friend...ain't never really had no true friend but you."*

Chapter 12: *"What had happened to T.J. in the night I did not understand, but I knew that it would not pass. And I cried or those things which had happened in the night and would not pass."*

Chapter 12: *"I cried for T.J. and the land."*

Conversation

Work in size-appropriate groups to write or perform the conversations that might have occurred in each of the following situations.

- Cassie tells her mother what happened with Little Man and the unwanted reading book. (2 people)

- Little Man tells Mama what happened to him on the first day of school. (2 people)

- Stacey and Cassie tell their Mama the truth about what they did to the school bus. (3 people)

- Cassie talks to Big Ma after her grandmother makes her apologize again to Lillian Jean Simms. (2 people)

- Uncle Hammer talks to Mr. Simms about Cassie's experience. (2 people)

- Lillian Jean talks to Jeremy about the way Cassie treated her. (2 people)

- Papa, Mr. Morrison, and Stacey talk on the way to Vicksburg. (3 people)

- Cassie asks her father if he set the fire. (2 people)

- R.W. and Melvin visit T.J. in jail. (3 people)

- Claude Avery talks to Stacey and Cassie on the first day of the new school year. (3 people)

- Cassie and her parents talk about what will happen to T.J. (3 people)

- Mr. Jamison talks to Cassie and Stacey about T.J. (3 people)

- Cassie tells her Mama about what happened with Lillian Jean. (2 people)

Bibliography of Related Reading

Fiction—Contemporary Life and Problems (Multicultural)

Anglo-American

Herlihy, Dirlie. *Ludie's Song.* (Cook,1980)

Hooks, William H. *Circle of Fire.* (Macmillan, 1982)

Spinelli, Jerry. *Maniac Magee.* (Little, 1990)

Waldron, Ann. *The Integration of Mary-Larkin Thornhill.* (Dutton, 1975)

Black-American

Armstrong, William H. *Sounder.* (Harper, 1962)

A sequel is *Sour Land* (Harper, 1971)

Bargar, Gary W. *Life Is Not Fair.* (Houghton, 1984)

Guy, Rosa. *The Ups and Downs of Carl Davis III.* (Delacorte, 1989)

Nichols, Joan Kane. *All but the Right Folks.* (Stemmer, 1985)

Taylor, Mildred. *The Friendship.* (Dial, 1987)

The Road to Memphis. (Dial, 1990) *Mississippi Bridge.* (Dial, 1990) *Let the Circle Be Broken.* (Dial, 1991)

Chinese-American

Lord, Bette Bao. *In the Year of the Boar and Jackie Robinson.* (Harper, 1984)

Yep, Laurence. *Child of the Owl.* (Harper, 1977)

Dragonwings. (Harper, 1975)

Hispanic-American

Hernandez, Irene Beltran. *Across the Great River.* (Arte Publico, 1989)

Mohr, Nicholas. *Felita.* (Dial, 1979)

Indian-American

Bosse, Malcolm. *Ganesh.* (Harper, 1981)

Jewish-American

Fiedler, Jean. *The Year the World Was Out of Step with Jancy Fried.* (Harcourt, 1981)

Marzollo, Jean. *Do You Love Me, Harvey Burns?* (Dial, 1983)

Neville, Emily. *Berries Goodman.* (Phillips, 1965)

Pfeffer, Susan Beth. *Turning Thirteen.* (Scholastic, 1988)

Japanese-American

Hamanka, Sheila. *The Journey.* (Watts, 1990)

Uchida, Yoshiko. *A Jar of Dreams.* (Macmillan, 1981)

Native-American

Chadwick, Roxane. *Don't Shoot.* (Lerner, 1978)

Dyer, T.A. *The Whipman is Watching.* (Watts, 1987)

Hale, Janet Campbell. *The Owl's Song.* (Avon, 1976)

Wallin, Luke. *Ceremony of the Panther.* (Macmillan, 1987)

Nonfiction

Ashabranner, Brent. *To Live in Two Worlds: American Indian Youth Today.* (Putnam, 1984)

Carson, Robert. *Mississippi.* (Children's Press, 1989)

Carpenter, Allan. *Enchantment of America: Mississippi.* (Regensteiener Publishing, 1978)

Daley, William. *The Chinese-Americans.* (Chelsea House, 1987)

Dolan, Edward F., *Jr. Anti-Semitism.* (Watts, 1985)

Garver, Susan, and Paula Mcguire. *Coming to North America from Mexico, Cuba, and Puerto Rico.* (Dell, 1981)

Katz, William Loren. *Black Indians: A Hidden Heritage.* (Macmillan, 1986)

Kitano, Harry. *Japanese Americans.* (Chelsea House, 1988)

Kranz, Rachel. *Straight Talk About Prejudice.* (Facts on File, 1992)

Lehrer, Brian. *The Korean Americans.* (Chelsea House, 1988)

Lester, Julius. *To Be A Slave.* (Dial, 1968)

McKissack, Patricia, and Frederick McKissack. *The Civil Rights Movement in America from 1865 to the Present.* (Childrens, 1987)

Meltzer, Milton. *The Hispanic Americans.* (Harper, 1982)

Naff, Alixa. *The Arab Americans.* (Chelsea House, 1988)

Selby, David. *Human Rights.* (Cambridge, 1987)

Spangler, Earl. *Blacks in America.* (Lerner, 1980)

Stanley, Marcia, Ed. *Better Homes and Gardens Beginner's Cookbook.* (Meredith, 1984)

Sterling, Dorothy. *Tear Down the Walls!* (Doubleday, 1968)

Warner, Margaret Brink and Ruth Ann Hayward, Comps. *What's Cooking? Favorite Recipes from Around the World.* (Little, 1981)

Winter, Frank H. *The Filipinos in America.* (Lerner, 1988)

Answer Key

Page 10

1. The four children are Stacey, 12; Cassie, 9; Christopher-John, 7; and Little Man, 6.

2. The Granger family sold it to a Yankee for tax money during the Reconstruction period. In 1887, it was up for sale and Grandpa Logan bought 200 acres. In 1918, he bought another 200 acres. The Logan family raises cotton.

3. The Logan family lives in Mississippi in 1933.

4. Papa must work a second job because the cotton crop is not bringing in enough money to pay for the mortgage and taxes on their land. He is now working in Louisiana, laying track for the railroads.

5. The bus driver enjoys making the black children run off the road and drenching them with dust or mud.

6. Little Man throws his school book because he sees on the inside cover what the Board of Education thinks of the black children.

7. Mama covers the offending inside cover with clean paper.

8. Mr. Morrison is a huge man, tall and muscular with deep life lines and partially gray hair. Papa brought Mr. Morrison to protect his family while he was away working for the railroad.

9. John Henry Berry was murdered by a white mob who set fire to him.

10. Stacey, Cassie, and their brothers dig a huge hole in the middle of the road; and since it is covered by standing water, the bus driver drives into it and the bus is severely damaged.

Page 15

1. Accept appropriate summaries.

2. The children find T.J. looking for the answers to a history test Mrs. Logan is going to give.

3. Stacey is angry about Mr. Morrison's presence because he feels that it is his job to protect the family while his father is away.

4. Stacey goes to the Wallace's store to find T.J. and beat him up for getting Stacey into trouble during the history test.

5. Mr. Morrison expects Stacey to prove he is a man by confessing to his mother that he went to the Wallace's and then taking his punishment.

6. Big Ma is proud of the way her late husband, Paul Edward, bought the land and was hard working. He also stood up to people and didn't let anyone take advantage of him.

7. Mama wanted the children to see how badly Mr. Berry had been burned and realize that since the Wallaces did it, their store was no place for them to be.

8. Cassie felt Mr. Jamison was like her father because he would always give you a straight answer. (Also, Cassie liked the lawyer because he was always respectful to her grandmother.)

9. Cassie becomes angry at Mr. Barnett because he ignores her, Stacey, and T.J., to wait on the white customers.

10. Big Ma makes Cassie apologize to Lillian Jean again so there will be no trouble. Big Ma doesn't want anything happening to her family.

Page 20

1. Accept appropriate summaries.

2. Stacey and Cassie think it is Mr. Granger's car. However, it turns out to be their Uncle Hammer's automobile.

3. Mama is afraid that if Uncle Hammer and Mr. Simms get into a fight, then the men who burned the Berrys might do the same thing to Hammer.

4. Mama tells Cassie that Mr. Simms believes that black people are not as good as whites. This makes him think he is more important.

5. T.J. makes Stacey think he looks bad in the coat. He teases Stacey to the point that Stacey gives him the coat, which is what T.J. wanted.

6. The Logans have a feast for Christmas. Some of the items on their menu include a raccoon cooked with onions, garlic and yams, ham, sweet-potato pie, egg-custard pies, and butter pound cakes.

7. Mr. Morrison tells the Logans that his sisters, mother and father were murdered by "night men" on Christmas when he was six.

8. The books might have been the first ones the children received that belonged only to them.

9. Jeremy was trying to apologize for the behavior of his father and sister in Strawberry. Jeremy liked the Logans and was trying to make friends with Stacey.

10. Mr. Jamison does not approve of what has been happening to the black people and wants to help them. Although he cannot put the Wallaces in jail he can help the black families shop in Vicksburg.

Answer Key *(cont.)*

Page 26

1. Accept appropriate summaries.

2. Lillian Jean is surprised when Cassie asks to carry her books since Cassie has never been friendly to her before.

3. Cassie's real reason for acting like a servant is to get revenge on Lillian Jean for acting as if she is better than Cassie.

4. Accept answers if acceptable reasons are given. Students may think it is a successful revenge since Lillian Jean is completely humiliated. Others may think it is not successful since Lillian Jean never understands the point of Cassie's actions.

5. T.J. is angry at Mrs. Logan for failing him for cheating. T.J. cannot accept responsibility for his own actions.

6. Kaleb Wallace and Harlan Granger's real reason for firing Mrs. Logan is to get back at the Logans for getting so many people to shop in Vicksburg.

7. Jeremy reports that his brothers, R.W. and Melvin are pretending to be friendly to T.J., but as soon as he is gone they call him names and make fun of him. Mama explains that some people use others to make them feel better about themselves.

8. Mr. Avery is a sharecropper on Mr. Granger's land. Mr. Granger told Mr. Avery that unless he starts shopping at the Wallace's store again, Mr. Granger will make them get off his land.

9. Papa is shot on the way back from Vicksburg and his leg is crushed when the wagon rolls over him.

10. Christopher-John and Little Man are afraid their father is going to die.

Page 31

1. Accept appropriate summaries.

2. Mr. Morrison first picks up the front and then the back of the truck and moves it far enough off the road for the wagon to pass.

3. One reason Jeremy probably spends so much time in the tree house is that he doesn't like, or get along with, his family.

4. Accept appropriate response. Some reasons Cassie likes the revival is the freedom the children have, there was so much food to eat, and it interrupted the "humdrum" routine of their lives.

5. Uncle Hammer sells his prize Packard automobile to help pay the mortgage.

6. Cassie felt sorry for T.J. because no one would talk to him at the meeting. He looked so unhappy and lonely.

7. Accept appropriate responses.

8. Mr. Jamison, the lawyer, was able to stop the Wallaces, for a little while, from killing T.J. and further hurting the other Averys.

9. Papa probably starts the fire in order to divert the mob from killing T.J. It was a way of stopping the mob without using a gun.

10. Cassie cries for T.J. because he may be imprisoned or killed unfairly. She is crying for the unfairness of her world where there is one law for whites and another for blacks.

Page 42

Matching

1. Little Man
2. T.J.
3. Papa
4. Jeremy
5. Mama
6. Mr. Jamison
7. Stacey
8. Cassie

True or False

1. False
2. False
3. True
4. True
5. True

Sequence 5 - 2 - 3 - 4 - 1

Paragraphs

1. Accept appropriate responses. Check that examples clearly support the writer's opinion.

2. Accept appropriate responses. Check to see that the writer uses examples that are from the novel.

Page 43

Accept all reasonable responses.

Page 44

Perform the conversations (dramas) in class. Ask students to respond to the conversations in several different ways, such as, "Are the conversations realistic?" or "Are the words the characters say in keeping with their personalities?"

Answer Key *(cont.)*

See page 5 for ways to use this picture.

48